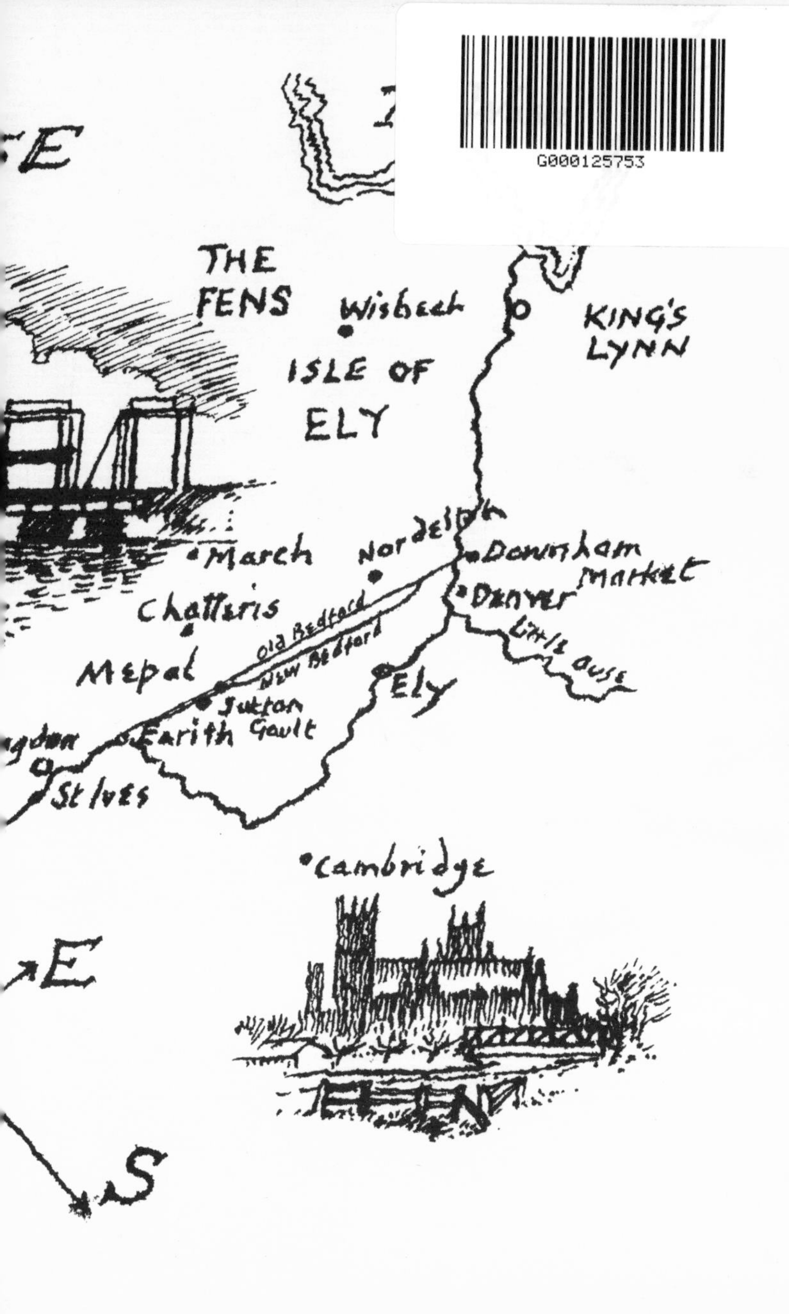
THE FENS
Wisbeach
KING'S LYNN
ISLE OF ELY
Nordelph
March
Downham Market
Chatteris
Denver
Old Bedford
New Bedford
Little Ouse
Mepal
Ely
Sutton Gault
Earith
St Ives
Cambridge
E
S

# The Great Ouse

Rivers • of • Britain

# The Great Ouse

## Fenland's Father

Wilson Stephens

*Illustrated by Gabriel White*

MULLER, BLOND & WHITE

The Introductory quotation is from St. Matthew's Gospel; that on page 44 is from *Say Not, the Struggle Naught Availeth* by Arthur Hugh Clough

First published in Great Britain in 1985 by
Muller, Blond & White Limited,
55 Great Ormond Street, London WC1N 3HZ.



British Library Cataloguing in Publication Data

Stephens, Wilson
The Great Ouse.—(Rivers of Britain)
1. Great Ouse, River (England)
I. Title II. White, Gabriel III. Series
942.6085'8 DA670.G7/

ISBN 0-584-11084-7

Printed and bound in Great Britain at The Bath Press, Avon

# Springhead

IN fact as well as in simile, a river expresses destiny. It shapes the fates of man and beast and bird. It gives fertility, life and movement to the countryside through which it flows. It sets human passions moving, such as devotion to homeland or envy of what others enjoy. Wise in their time, ancient peoples believed rivers to be animate, each possessing its own soul.

This could well be true of the Great Ouse, in the sense that what has happened to it, and around it, has so involved the people of its region that they have given their own identity to it in the manner of a reflection. Were it not for the Great Ouse, the Fens, the fen folk, their prosperity and way of life could not have existed. From this single river has been created a distinctive English region, immensely prosperous; and, more important, a self-aware community of the English people, true to their unfolding history, different in traditions and attitude, and proud of the difference.

This is one of a series of river studies. Its aim is to identify the spirit of the Great Ouse which has spread over those great tracts which cover most of East Anglia, and where there are no such things as hills. Instead, plenty of room for wonder, and an elusive magic for those who learn to find it.

*What went ye forth for to see?*
*A reed shaken with the wind?*

# The Great Ouse

WHERE the Great Ouse flows, the sky is the limit. Elsewhere ours is an island of small outlooks. Crests enclose most of our views; inland, the sight of a true horizon is rare and to stretch our eyes generally impossible. Seldom can we see more than ten miles before hills or woodlands enclose the scene. Not for us the uplift which comes from day-long journeys through the ever-retreating distances of the world's great land spaces, the Indian plains, the North American prairies or the Russian steppes — unless we are in the Fens.

Here the sun rises at eye-level. No higher ground intervenes to mask the moment of dawn. At evening the sun goes down at eye-level, ruddy in the cooling vapours, with nothing to hide the instant of its dipping out of sight.

The land begins and ends in nothing as far away as we can see. The clouds sail across it, spaced out in fleet-formation. Behind them the fenland sky is azure in summer, ice-blue in winter, sometimes iron-grey with storm or snow. It is the widest and most magnificent or most awesome sky in Britain, worthy to be called what the Bible calls it, a firmament.

Beneath it the harvests are heavy all the year round with corn, sugar-beet, fruit, and market garden crops. In winter, when the land rests, it may be rich brown loam or the black alluvial left where thousands of years' growth of reeds and rushes have died and rotted into mould.

For mile after mile the roads run above the level of the fields, and the fields lie below the level of the sea. Here and there they are patched or streaked by grey-green rushes. Nodding kecksies and reed mace show where primeval fen has defied all efforts to tame it, or they trace the line of river or drain across the landscape, its banks still clad as the whole region formerly was. Endlessly the wind sweeps across this open plain, mild from the softer England to the west and south, salt-laden from the north and east so that fen folk can never forget the sea, their neighbour and long-time enemy.

Our eyes and ears tell us that this immense plain is a different land; different from what it was, different

from the higher ground around it. The theme of its bird voices is not the coo of wood pigeon or songs of warblers and finches but the free liquid cries of redshank, sandpiper and other birds of marsh and foreshore. The sky is patterned often by formations of duck in flight — mallard families, wisps of teal, great airborne rafts of wigeon.

When the fenland perspective becomes less new, the visitor's eye grows practised enough for glimpses of the towns and villages to be less elusive, though they are seemingly flattened in the wide scene. Their majestic churches and not less assertive red brick chapels, where the singing recalls negro spirituals, proclaim it as a land of God-fearing people, of Bunyan and the Wesleys, as well as the prince-bishops of Ely and Peterborough.

The psalm singers of past years must have seen irony in the words, "the earth is the Lord's and all that therein is". For here the sky is the Lord's, and the earth man-made. It was rescued from desolation by muscle-cracking feats of reclamation which worked outwards from either bank of the Great Ouse river. Fen folk saw their whole world changed by the hands of men.

Only three centuries have passed since the Fens were a secret land, the watery desert which their name describes. Tracts of lagoon and wastes — windswept, wild, chill, mist-hung, inimical — they had been abandoned by all except scattered families of the marsh men who clung with bloody-minded tenacity to an unfriendly terrain which nobody else wanted, and which the sea periodically reoccupied.

In ten human generations that wilderness has become Britain's most productive soil, most of its people richer than other regional communities, vigorous in physique and outlook to the point of prizing as an honour their own minatory epithet, the tigers. Fenland is the Texas of Britain, where folk see themselves as a head higher than any others, and where life is lived at work and play with non-stop vigour.

This flat land has been the creation of a people blessed with a belated vision, and a habitat based on fidelity to simple principles, spiritual as well as material, comparable to the Pilgrim Fathers in America. It is one of England's great success stories. And when its human element turn from psalms to hymns and sing as they often do, "Shall we gather at the river" the Great Ouse is in their minds.

The Ouse, the fenland artery, is the third greatest English river, a majestic waterway which three quarters of the nation forget and most of the rest under-estimate. A possible reason is that soon after the Great Ouse reaches maturity it becomes a perquisite of the fen men, so for anybody else to claim a shared interest in it seems near impertinence.

Ouse, that descriptive word, says exactly what it means — not a trickle, but slow-moving. It applies to other English rivers too. Hence the Great, to distinguish this Ouse from its namesake of the plain of York, a lesser Ouse but still a major river; from the Little Ouse which flows into the Great across fenland from the Norfolk Breck, a route that gives not much more fall than a billiard table; and from the Sussex Ouse which saunters out of the Wealden forests and, surprisingly, attracts one of the best sea-trout runs in southern Britain.

Nature made the Great Ouse only one of the fenland rivers, others being the Nene, the Welland and the Witham. But man made it the main artery of a whole region. For centuries all their lower reaches wandered through the limitless reed beds, often indistinguishable from the idle floodwater around them, yet somehow collecting and conveying all the run-off from the Midland hills to the sea.

In those past ages southerly winds blew over virtually nothing but reeds from Cambridge to Lincoln. The western boundary of fenland still runs roughly parallel and a few miles east of the Great North Road. Between it and the sea the billowing reed tops made a visual sea of their own.

Bending and straightening to the gusts, they set up their own rolling wave pattern. In the grey but mobile desolation, tough, secretive, independent Englishmen went their hidden ways, chiefly by punting themselves between the dry spots where villages had been set up, minding their own business and living hard. Their sense of belonging to their own scene kept them separate from the upland communities to the west.

In the open now, with richness where the marshes lay, their descendants still have their sense of being a race apart. In colloquial speech, they are Yellow-bellies to the rest of Britain. The title has been preserved, in no deprecatory sense, in that rough storehouse of folklore, the Army.

Perhaps it originated in a uniform once worn by a fenland regiment; perhaps it alludes to the frogs which still croak through the summer nights from fields bounded by fenland dikes. Whatever the origin, and whether by battalions or singly, Yellowbellies they remain to outside folk, though among themselves they are fen tigers. Either title reflects the self-confidence and the communal morale of people who, albeit tardily and unwillingly, banded together and made something out of what was virtually nothing.

# The Gentlemen Adventurers

THERE was not much banding together when the idea of draining the Fens was new, except to resist what their forefathers saw as encroachment of the fen folk's life style. They took the traditional English view, that any change is for the worse. Over many generations they had adapted to their sea of reeds. More than a thousand years had passed since a Roman attempt at reclamation was abandoned.

In the early seventeenth century, when King and Parliament were falling out and Cromwell was to rule the land, the fen dwellers were safely insulated from political storms. Nobody envied them, few strangers came, armies kept clear. In their thatched cottages of daub-and-wattle, little different from those of the Saxon settlers from whom they were descended, grouped into villages and small towns supplied by sea rather than overland, they could well ride that storm as they had ridden out so many others.

Hereward the Wake had set the fashion, defying William the Conqueror for years after the rest of England surrendered. Thereafter anybody who for public or private reasons wished to fade away, temporarily or permanently beyond range of publicity, could always do so under the fenland mists. Those already under them valued their spartan freedoms, recoiled from touching forelocks to sovereign, nobleman or squire, and saw self-employment, however hand to mouth, as better than working for others.

So what was the Earl of Bedford (as the title then was) doing in 1630 when he formed his company which bore the ominous designation of the Gentlemen Adventurers? Those words in themselves were enough to polarise resistance from the forerunners of the fen tigers, who did not hold with gentlemen.

What the Earl of Bedford proposed was as simple in concept as it was enormous in undertaking. By straightening its course and accelerating its flow he intended to make the Great Ouse, the river of the county which bore his name, draw the surplus out of the waterlogged fens, and take it to the sea.

The land it left would be rich beyond anybody's dreams. The Earl and his Gentlemen Adventurers backed his vision with their money, and hired the Dutchman Cornelius Vermuyden to put something better in the place of the sea of reeds.

The fen folk gave Vermuyden more than his fair share of non-cooperation. It was a digging job, and they were not for it, nor were they attracted by the declared objectives. They had a strong suspicion that whoever else became richer as a result, they would not. They believed that the Gentlemen Adventurers were laying out cash for their own benefit, not for the sake of anybody else.

The marsh men were both right and wrong. The landowners, the only people who could have set up

the scheme, profited initially; had they not done so, it would not have been financed. The wider benefit took time, but we now know that the newly released riches have long since percolated through all the social strata. Although it is still possible to be poor in the Fens, it has also been possible for a great many not very privileged people to become very rich indeed.

Like most great undertakings, it had its initial razor's edge. Since the locals would not put in a hand's turn, others had to be found. They came from varied sources. Scottish prisoners of war were brought in by the thousand. The workhouses of England disgorged every able-bodied inmate.

The work was not only done, but much of it was done twice or more. The men of the marshes did not all stand idly by. Some proved industrious saboteurs.

The result was a different face of Nature. New water channels, direct as airport runways, linked the inland fens to the distant sea. First success came incredibly quickly. Vermuyden was knighted before he was 35. As is the way of things, he was soon forgotten as land values soared where acres had previously changed hands for peppercorns. He died in London, in obscurity, and in a parlous financial plight.

The extent of the reclaimed area is most evident on modern maps. The village of Fowlmere, a tell-tale name, marks its southern limit. The parish is in Cambridgeshire but beyond its southern boundary lies Hertfordshire with all its modern connotations of London's environs. Northward, the grid system of delphs and drains continues up to Wragby, beyond Lincoln, with another arm of reclaimed fen lying between wolds and sea as far as the Humber.

Eastward the tofts of Thetford in Norfolk, alias tufts, were once the first islands of dry land and still mark the farther limit of the former primeval marsh. Westward the village of Stilton, home of the famous Leicestershire cheese, overlooks Peterborough and the flat lands stretching out of sight.

This great quadrilateral enclosed a region, still more self-contained than the counties composing it, in which the thinly-scattered population evolved their own brand of self-reliance and independence. Their life was hand-to-mouth. The fens produced little else but reeds for thatching, withies for basket-making, and fowl for such markets as could be reached.

For the locals there were fish in the rivers, and enough dry patches to grow grain for bread and gruel. Beyond that, each man used his hunting skills to keep himself and his family alive. It was a survival economy. To grow rich was unthinkable, and a fat man impossible.

Hence the significance of Fowlmere, and the recurrence in fenland place names of the word Decoy. Human life in the fens depended on the exploitation of wild birds. In the days before gunpowder they caught birds for food just as they caught fish, by netting them. The netting took sophisticated forms. When the gun superceded the net, the term fowling piece emerged for weapons used by commercial rather than sporting shooters. They were used with great skill and few ethics.

The acme of fenland bird netting was the decoy. This was a large, well camouflaged system of nets enclosing an area the size of a tennis court and supported on a permanent wooden framework, into which the birds were funnelled through ever-narrowing channels, also netted on both sides and overhead. Some decoys were operated for centuries and three were still being worked after the second World War, the objective then being to obtain birds for research, not for poulterers' shops.

The decoy process demanded close knowledge of the ways of ducks and geese. Where the word decoy survives, as it does in Cambridgeshire, Suffolk,

Norfolk and Lincolnshire — sometimes on maps and signposts, sometimes as field names or in local speech — the lie of land and water would once have made the enterprise possible.

The first problem was to choose a site which would attract edible species only, not that much was inedible to fenmen themselves in times of dearth. But distant customers were choosy, and enormous as the bird populations of the pre-drainage fens were, they had to be marketed selectively.

The wind-tossed sea of reeds was full of life. But geese are too wary to be decoyed; few of the waders would find buyers; heron and bittern would give alarm too soon. The problem was to separate the ducks, in particular the ducks which customers most favoured, from the rest.

An area of reed-fringed shallow water would be chosen, a fowl mere in fact, to which flighting duck could be baited in, attracted by rotten fodder roots or mouldy grain, and by semi-domesticated call ducks which enticed them down. Concealed among high reeds and sallow trees, the decoy itself was constructed at one end.

Silence was the essence of the manoeuvre while decoy men watched for days, perhaps for weeks, as duck numbers on the mere or decoy pond built up. Shallow water attracted the dabbling species — mallard, wigeon, teal, shoveller and garganey — which are more popular on plates than the diving and sea-duck which tend to taste of fish.

At last the time would come to move the birds toward the funnel, and thence into the decoy itself.

Easy enough to move duck into the air, with that great clappering which leaves the sky briefly winking with the whitened flashings of a thousand underwings; very difficult, even with all possible skill and luck, to move swimming birds very gently forward, concentrating them in the tactical area at the mouth of the funnel, and then to make them swim into it.

The critical moment was when the first of them swam between the nets. Men on the banks, men in boats, stealthily pressed the round-up forward, well aware that ducks have a psychological weakness. It is curiosity.

A dog, small and brown and white for choice, was trained to act as attractor. Its role was to scamper playfully on the bank, disappearing and reappearing among the rushes beside the netted funnel; just near enough to set the ducks wondering what it was, too far away to scare them, gradually retreating towards the main decoy, acting as a pied piper to the swimming ducks.

Soon a large, garrulous mob of them would follow it. Other ducks, anxious not to miss the fun, would jostle to join them. Soon a crowd instinct took command, the normally wary birds abandoned caution, and the funnel became crammed with its one-way traffic, for which there was no escape.

When they were inside, the decoy was closed. The birds could be kept there, if undisturbed and well-fed, for days on end to catch a favourable market. A successfully run decoy, across the years, caught hundreds of thousands of duck.

# Punt Guns and Dawn Mist

THE water's recession reduced the ducks' inland feeding areas. When corn crops instead of reeds eventually bowed and straightened to the wind, men and women in greater number moved on to the land — ploughing, sowing, reaping and binding, loading the harvest and gleaning the empty fields. Villages expanded to take in the growing labour force, new settlements formed on land won back from water, the former wilderness held more and more people.

They broke the solitude that had made the decoys possible at a density comparable to that of the windmills that replaced them. Simultaneously, the fowl meres were drying out as the water was drawn away to the distant river and down it to the sea. Instead of the duck coming to human neighbourhoods, the fowlers had to go in search of duck, ever deeper into the remaining fens, ever farther from their homes.

Those were the years of the gun's emergence as a food procurement instrument. There was nothing elegant, no sporting chivalry towards the quarry behind that transition. The time had yet to come for shooting to be a gentlemen's recreation.

The fowling piece was a harvesting implement no less than the sickle or, in some cases, the modern

combine-harvester. The ball-firing musket of the Civil War armies was almost innocuous beside the seventeenth century's 'harquebuss or blanterbuss' adopted for use against flocks of duck or indeed geese, for now the professional market-hunters had a means which, unlike the net, operated also on the foreshores.

Designed to fire scatter-shot in patterns, these weapons could be made to fire much else. They were muzzle loaders, and the projectiles rammed down on to the powder charge were as varied as the resources and imaginations of the fenmen themselves.

Pulverised scrap of many forms, nails, bolt heads, even pebbles sieved to size, all served to fill the air with death above parties of feeding duck shot on the

water or at the moment of flushing. It was a bloody, merciless and unlovely business, in principle little different from the massacre of the bison on the prairies, ruthless as any predation of hungry humanity on Nature.

Of course, it needed mastery of the many problems in stalking creatures as alert, cunning and cautious as wild duck. The art of bringing gun and birds together survived in the practice of punt-gunning which continued among professional fowlers until restricted by the Countryside Act of 1982. Most fowlers had long since become part-timers by then; all of them are primarily guides nowadays; none mass-killers. But here and there the ancient skill was reactivated when conditions favoured or necessitated it, and is still not wholly illegal. A lonely scene, an ancient cunning; small wonder that its challenge has been slow to die, long outliving its economic need.

A fowler's skiff, its mere inch or two of freeboard making it little more visible to swimming duck than a floating plank, would ease through the swatches between the reed beds, under the mist of a freezing dawn. The gunner lay in the bilge, facing forward, only enough of his well-muffled face above gunwale-level to give him a view ahead.

That way he could see enough to stalk a raft of duck on open water when they settled to preen and sleep after feeding through the night. That way, too, he could sight his gun. This, four-bore or larger, still has a legal maximum of one and a half inches calibre.

Already loaded, fixed to fire directly forward, aiming it was by lining the boat on to the target. The fowler's hands, gloved for camouflage, were overside to port and starboard. Each deftly and silently operated a very small paddle to give both way and steering. Speed was not needed; stealth all important.

Latterly, at the end of the centuries-long process of controlling the water, punt-gunning has been possible only in the remaining areas where fens reach out to the sea. It exercised a bygone tactic, generally carried out only to prove that the skills behind it had not died. It was always strictly for hardy men who knew their waters, their waterfowl, their boats, their weather and their guns.

When a shot was fired, never more often than once per sortie, the element of hazard was not confined to the ducks. The gun's considerable recoil could be absorbed only by the craft itself, which might be driven backwards several times its own length. If the shot succeeded there were calls on effective dogwork in gathering the bag, and on watermanship in navigating home with an extra load.

So a relic of the past survived into our own age. Not perhaps the most attractive bequest of history to sport, it remains an undeniable link between the human values in the centuries of the sea of reeds and those in the latter day centuries of corn, sugar, and vegetables. The decoy men and the wildfowlers were a relentless brotherhood, fiercely individualistic, physically very tough; among them no quality was more respected than masculine strength.

They ruled the fens, and they survived the fens because they knew and loved so well that strange, wild, wide, wet, flat land for ever under the sweeping wind which carried with it the free, rippling cries of birds of the open spaces. They understood it in darkness as well as by day, in those black and silent nights when the luminous marsh gas rose and its ghostly jack o'lanterns flitted among the reed-girt islands.

Their descendants, inheriting the qualities which made that survival possible, and the knowledge that their forefathers learned and handed down, well express those formative influences. They have a stiff but unassertive pride in themselves.

What would be a feat for other people, a fen tiger reckons to do as a matter of course. They have a great capacity for holding to a chosen course. They know good luck when they see it, and make the most of it. They expect nothing without effort, accepting that he who demands something from life must turn to, use his hands and sense, and earn it.

They are an enclosed community still, speaking their distinctive dialect, its elongated vowels often incomprehensible to strangers ("Gwyn Naarge mahrer" means "I'm going to Norwich tomorrow"). Their inborn, unsentimental feel for Nature is a marketable commodity today. Since the Fens breed gamekeepers as Wales breeds Rugby footballers that strange speech has become the lingua franca of the job. So the bird lore of the decoys and the fowling skiffs lives on with those for whom it is bred in the bone.

# Sluice, Pump and Lode

THE affinity of fen people with the river which has shaped and re-shaped their countryside is total, the converse only half true. Fenland — its straightened, efficient, utilitarian channels streamlined to their purpose — is a far contrast from the Ouse of Middle England, where it earns its distinctive Great. Paradoxically, the more the Ouse grows the less it dominates its landscape, eventually almost losing its broad strong-flowing self, seeming a mere thread of water dwarfed in the sweeping vista it reclaimed.

On the high spine of the South Midlands, the corn and beef country where Buckinghamshire and Northamptonshire meet, the Ouse serves its apprenticeship as a brook, trickling along not far from the motor-racing circuit at Silverstone. It has become a recognisable river at Buckingham town. Then it loses itself in the fast-growing ramifications of Milton Keynes, emerging in splendid flow, wide and peaceful as it crosses Bedfordshire's fertile miles.

In better days than these (but days which, with luck, will return for our descendents) the Ouse was paramount among elm tree rivers. The elms' great height, their graceful crowns bowing regally, and the freshness of their rippling leaves gave life and depth and perspective to all its far-flung vale.

Spaced along its banks, the scenic character they created was shared by no other trees — until the larvae of a Dutch beetle killed them and, for safety's sake, axes laid low the standing corpses. Only the humbler sallows were left to trace the Ouse's course. Poor substitutes, they lack the element of majesty.

But elm is a tough, tenacious, thoroughly English tree. Where many of the once soaring boles lie thrown, dried out and grey in death, young suckers, pliant as withies in these years of grace, are already springing from their deep root stocks. How long, how long? Not my generation, nor the next, but perhaps the generation after that will see them sturdy-trunked and fifty-foot tall, swaying again to the English wind, their branches' tracery veining the grey cloudscapes of English winters.

At Bedford eight-oared racing shells can take each other on, blade to blade across the broadening Ouse. In the intervening miles the river has seemed conscious of its growing image, determined to parade it by visiting as many towns and villages as possible. So circuitous is its course that it could serve as a campaign route for election candidates.

Beyond Bedford the flat vale, long ago the drainage channel of yet earlier fens left behind when the Roman withdrawal let in the sea to re-occupy their earlier reclamation, enabled the weight of water coming down to straighten the present Ouse's natural course, first north through St. Neots to Huntingdon, then east to St. Ives and Earith. At that misty, once water-girt township the hand of man supercedes the forces of Nature.

Downstream, Dutch-named villages lie alongside English; the waters, now controlled, are categorised in Dutch terms. The fact of fenland, the flat and boundless plain replacing the roll of the landscape which is otherwise the face of England, duplicates the Low Countries scenery across the neighbouring sea.

From Earith the main attack was launched on the stagnant waters and the reed beds. A new ruler-straight channel was dug for the two Ouse rivers, the Great and the Little (sometimes known as the Old West River) which joins there. It runs for twenty miles to Denver, near Downham Market, site of the sluices at the culmination of the system which lifted the fenlands above water level. The new waterway was named the Old Bedford River. It did half the necessary job, changing the fens from marshland to pasture which could be used for the drier months of each year.

But if winter was also to be won for cultivation of corn and other crops, the rate of water expulsion had to be doubled. So another channel was made, parallel with the first and half a mile from it, and called the New Bedford River. Today it is sometimes known more prosaically as the Hundred Foot Drain. It, too, ended at Denver where the sluices and lodes allowed the water thus gathered to run on into the sea at King's Lynn, and prevented it running back.

# The Face of the Waters

THUS began a three century long war between man and water. At first the fen folk scoffed, declaring that the water would always win in the end. Many things happened, each of which seemed to prove them right, each of which was countered by some new extraction or defence work, for soon the war was on two fronts — against the inland water and against the sea.

As land values increased in response to new productivity, more and more fenmen began to see the outcome in terms of their own prosperity. As their old life style faded into history, they joined in the fight for the future.

Now the sea was not only the old enemy, but the worst enemy. Though the Ouse was the main river, it was not the only line of exit for water from the fens, nor the only point of counter-attack by the tides. The land water had not only to be gathered up and led away; it had to be disposed of.

The only disposal area was and is the Wash, that shallow, sand-barred inlet, with its thirty miles of uninhabited coast at the mercy of wind and tide, still a mystery except to those born and bred to its tricky frontier of saltings, gutters and mud-flats. There the wild geese come in winter, sea-duck and land duck meet and mingle, while wheeling flocks of knot, dunlin, sanderling, plover and other wading birds

load the changing winds with the wild music of their voices.

The other major rivers flow out here. These are the Nene and the Welland. The former is the Ouse's partner to the north. They flow side by side, about twenty miles apart, across the grain of Middle England. The Welland comes in after winding its way through those fens which lie in Lincolnshire. Combined, the water volume carried by them is always great.

In winter, when rain has saturated not only the fens but the higher ground behind them too, the force of the landwater discharged into the Wash becomes enormous. The three rivers run bank high. The Ouse brings down a double burden in its twin channels, the

Old and New Bedford rivers, side by side, like gun-barrels, aimed with their ever-increasing force at the Denver sluices. If the wind turns north-easterly, building up the tides of the Wash, nowhere is left for the water to go — except to spread over the fens where it came from, where it lay undisturbed for so many centuries and where folk have long said it belongs.

The Denver sluices then become a vast control valve. They maintain a crucial balance, holding back river floodwater from inundating the thirty-miles of fens downstream, and relieving the pressure on the banks of the artificial waterways upstream. Thus they are the key point in the preservation of Britain's richest food-producing area.

In the second World War it was known that the

Germans were well aware of this. If they could have bombed the Denver sluices, or landed paratroops to blow them up as they had plans to do, they could have destroyed a major element of our self-support. While docks, naval bases, airfields and armament factories were most in the news, these drainage and flood defence installations, remote in the lonely flatlands, were among the first of our vulnerable points to be placed under secrecy and guarded by troops.

In the event, the Germans never attacked; they knew they had lost the element of surprise. And the Royal Air Force turned the tables on them. The dambusters' raid achieved the effect in Germany that the Germans had planned for Denver, by inundating the Ruhr instead.

Across the years, from the first efforts of the Earls of Bedford and of Vermuyden onwards, Nature fought back as Nature always does, wreaking recurrent havoc. Every ten years or so either the sea walls or the river banks gave way.

Between Denver and the Wash is that thirty-mile-wide strip of reclaimed fen. Across it the last of the major river works, the Flood Relief channel, enables the sluices to act as a traffic control for the outgoing waters. An uneasy peace has been achieved.

But in living memory that peace has not always held. When a high tide, driven into the great cul-de-sac of the Wash by a north-easterly gale, coincided with heavy rain and a rising load of landwater racing down the new channels, something often had to give. Then the sturdy, stout-hearted water-wise locals would be joined by soldiers in the urgent task of laying sandbags to raise the banks and to keep the rampant Ouse inside its bed, the sea outside its defences, or both.

The defenders would be urged on through the drenching, storm-torn nights by the roar of water over the sluices, its sonorous crescendo an awesome threat. Men toiled. Women kept up everlasting supplies of hot food and tea. Many a parson prayed. Generally the combined efforts were enough. Sometimes they were not.

They failed in 1953, at the start of Coronation year. What happened then was unforgettable for those who saw it, especially those who lived through it, fighting for survival in and around their own homes as the fen tigers of bygone centuries had done. I was a visitor, a

recorder of other people's ordeal.

What that was, visualised now, may be dismissed as a past misfortune as inconsequential to us as are the war experiences of a past generation. Be warned. In Nature, nothing happens for the last time. What happened then is not impossible now even if flood defences are maintained at their present level; it is a certainty if they are not.

In that devastation only thirty years ago the Fens were not a sea of reeds, as they would have been in the further past. They were a world of naked water rampaging uncontrolled, the sea and rivers mixed, whipped up by a rasping wind under the gun-metal grey of the winter sky. We went by police launch across the drowned fields and roads, to villages where their white walls were darkened by the universal wet, their garden trees bowed submissively under the blast, dipping branches in the racing water that made every land a river.

From marooned farms and stricken cottages, rescue boats plied to and fro. Housewives climbed aboard expressionless, suddenly redundant. Some cradled babies. Husbands and fathers had sterner work to do. Old men and women sat grey-featured amid bundles and suitcases.

None looked to where they were going; all faced back, speechlessly, towards the homes they had left. The atmosphere was not of escape, but of abandonment; not of anger, but of resignation at what, in their deep instincts, every fen dweller knew could happen, and can happen again.

Drowned sheep, pigs, occasional bullocks drifted

past, bloated, all four legs in the air. Gulls rode the wind miles inland, their cold eyes down-looking for floating garbage. Fenland fields are generally bounded by water-filled dikes, so hedges are few. But here and there lines of leafless thorns broke surface. On one such bush a pair of partridges perched (the only partridges I have ever seen do so), miserable in the searing wind, no dry land in sight, but inseparable from their native soil four feet under the water.

So we navigated by outboard motor from town to town, always wary of the racing currents which marked the course of the drains and delphs below still leading water back to the Ouse, but making no visible impression yet. In the little towns fenland's fighting spirit reacted characteristically to emergency. The local folk were concentrating all of it on winning the kind of battle against water which made them what they are, with the energy which in better times still fires the intense vitality of fenland life.

Drive along fenland roads, stand in a fenland street drinking in the atmosphere, live a while with fen people, do a little business with them. There is no hanging around at work or at play. This is where men get going, and keep going. When the peril is past, life goes purposefully on.

Great articulated box cars burn up the miles along the straight flat roads faster than anywhere in Britain, their drivers heading inland with go-getters' sense of urgency. They come from North Sea ports loaded with Euro-imports, or from farms and markets with corn or beasts or vegetables for London and other conurbations, from far stretching fields with cargoes of beet for the sugar factories.

Wherever, whatever, or whoever, the pressing-on is the same. There is an impulsion which makes fen life resemble the New World rather than the rest of Britain. Other similarities relate causes to effects.

As the Ouse development changed the face and character of its hinterland, the Fens became a colonisation, contemporaneously with America and like it in miniature. The new country which was being created gave its people new attitudes. Man had won a war against Nature. There were fortunes to be made, frontiers to be pushed back — frontiers of reeds and water.

The beginnings were raw, the rewards great. The people who resulted were self-reliant, self propelled. Families strengthened each other by mutual help. A new coherence grew up, binding the whole region together. There was not, and is not, much scope for airs and graces outside the Cambridge colleges and the ecclesiastical enclaves. The brusque, to-the-point, fenland manner developed.

The emergent tradition of all new countries is one of classlessness. This remains true in the Fens. There are indeed great landlords, but they are less in evidence than their tenants. There are employers and employees, but they do not differ greatly. The fen landscape includes them all in its own great levelling process.

On the black soil of the once well-named Soke of Peterborough and the Isle of Ely the uncompromisingly plain red-brick houses stand up square and

stark, spaced regularly, acres apart across the flat land that seems to have no ending. The black soil has fortunes locked in it for those with the strength of arm and the know-how to unlock it. Only a few acres of it, zealously worked, can mean prosperity.

Fen folk do not express their prosperity by grandeur. A dwelling and a barn is all they need while the year turns around them. Winter's downpours and icy winds, Spring's hardly less chilling sunshine, Summer's harvest weather and Autumn's gale-swept foretaste of another Winter, all come and go round these unprotected homes.

Trees for windbreak are rare, sheltered places non-existent in that wide defenceless plain where only laboriously piled bog oak trunks give a lea to out-wintering cattle. To the eye, it is a scene of unrelieved starkness and long odds against which to live.

Yet those plain homes, bludgeoned by gales, are havens of warmth and good cheer when their doors close on rough weather outside. Then the enduring fen tradition of comfort, nurtured in adversity, takes over. Living in Britain's least sheltered zone, fen people have become masters in the art of living well.

# The Land of the Tigers

DESPITE the fertility around them, and the protective effects of modernity, the outdoor lives of the fen people remain by any standards harsh for months on end. This results not only from the open terrain and its defencelessness against the Arctic breath of weather from the north and east, but from the ways in which their money is made. Acre for acre the real turn-over comes from market garden crops.

Unlike the grain and root production of arable farming, there is a limit to the mechanisation of vegetable growing. It stays labour-intensive, demanding outdoor skills which are both manual and precise. Much of its is women's work (and no cant about equal opportunity).

Women as well as men work the land, braving winter at its most bitter, summer at its most exhausting, when a ten-hour day in a heat-wave makes the Fens seem not very different from the Sahara, and overtime far removed from a fringe benefit. Men do the heavy jobs of ploughing and cultivation, transportation, and using machinery; women the detailed plantsmanship, often kneeling or bent double, deft fingers performing operations at a speed that nothing artificial can equal.

Growing celery, for instance. The celery that is eaten nationwide nearly all comes from the fens. The soil here is ideal for its mass production. But celery, as gardeners know, is a chancy crop in its early stages.

The germination of its seed is an odds-against gamble, the survival of the seedlings an hourly anxiety. So ninety per cent of Britain's celery begins its short life in vast glasshouses at Whittlesey near Peterborough, a village which lives for celery, where by dispensation of Providence the soil and the atmosphere combine as nowhere else to make its propogation a near-certainty in experienced hands.

These are the hands of the women who, after the initial seed-burst, prick out the tiny plants for growing-on in the open. Crawling on earth that is no more alluring than any other despite its fertility, they work at a rate of 25,000 transplants per woman per day. A few weeks later all are lifted again and sold to farmers throughout the Fens for re-planting on a field scale for market.

All across the wide flat land are similar specialities, similar dexterities, similar sustained effort by the folk who go down on their knees for their living on the black gold of fen soil over which their ancestors waded or walked on stilts in days gone by.

This background of hard toil, of literally getting down to it, has given fen people their relatively high-earnings life style. Out of the roistering wind and the parching sun has come the zest for replenishment which puts the tiger into fen physiology.

Intensity of effort is balanced by wholeheartedness in thirst and hunger. Fen appetites are among the wonders of British life. He is a bold man who essays to match pints with tigers; and a plate with any segment of the rim not covered by food is a mark of shame to the mistress of the household. In a land of plenty, they eat plenty, work it off by energetic social life and manliness in recreation.

Either the weather or the opposition, or both, must be withstood in everything a fen man does. This is no place for softies, nor ever was. It is no accident that such small towns as Chatteris, March and Wisbech have so proud a record in producing boxers.

There have been boxers in a special fen tradition in which the ring is not the place for refinements like the noble art of self defence, but rather for forthright attack and demolition of the other fellow in the positive fen manner. Over the names of Boon and Green and Sadd hangs the shade of Oliver Cromwell, who behaved likewise in greater matters. A fenman too, he was aware from infancy that thrice blessed is he who gets his blow in first.

Out of doors, inevitably, the sports of the Fens are for hardy men. When rain has drummed through moonless nights in an early winter, fens long-drained are flooded again and rich land returns to what it was, mere and mud. If frost follows the shallow waters freeze easily and may be locked solid for weeks. Then the years roll away as skates come out, and fen folk of all ages and each gender return to their ancestors' mode of winter transport.

In times past, skates brought new mobility to the fens for as long as a freeze-up lasted. The drains and cuts and other man-made waterways linked towns and villages with routes as straight as Roman roads along which skaters could average twenty miles an hour self-propelled, not much slower than a modern bus. To the thrill of speed was added the fun of family reunions otherwise impossible except at great cost in the days of coach or train. The fen man or woman who could not skate was a rarity.

There the modern steel-bladed skate is still comparatively new. For centuries pattens, wooden keels lashed to shoes or boots, were the traditional way of fast winter travel. Only racers used steel.

Universal car ownership has ended the need for accelerated pedestrianism and brought indoor ice rinks within everybody's reach. Nevertheless the urge to skate, and especially to race, under natural conditions is still overwhelming. When the ice is good spectators in thousands come out to watch the speed men in action on the traditional racing meres of Hilgay and Cowbit fens and many more.

As these and others like them became dry for most of the year when the Ouse and its man-made parallels gradually sucked their waters away and crops replaced the surrounding reed-beds, their duck populations moved outwards toward the coast. Land and sea merge in a miles-wide strip of saltings across which, twice daily, "far back, through creeks and inlets making, comes silent, flooding in, the main" and wildfowl gather in their own lost world.

Half sea, half land, in turns shrouded in mists, darkened by driving storms or lit by celestial sunshine, this is where land runs out, water runs in, and on their ever-changing meeting ground men trust their lives to their instincts and wits. The roaring winds which sweep across it in winter come from Russia or the Pole. The tides make and ebb, creeping with uncanny speed across mud-flats, gurgling up and down the gutters. Man or beast which moves too late, or moves wrongly, invites the fate of being islanded or drowned; quite often the sea, forever cruel, accepts the invitation.

Where Ouse runs out is a far contrast with its beginnings on the high, dry spine of England, in the dignity of oak woods and ancient parks where pheasants cock-up and rooks caw. Here there are wilder voices.

The voices of the wader flocks, their lean wings swinging them under the wind; the jabber of ducks peaceful at their day-long rest; the changing voices of the grey wild geese finding even in this bleak scene a refuge from the pitiless north, flying inland by day to scavenge potato fields where their forebears grazed between the meres.

This is where, winter-long, the wildfowlers come. Hardy men impervious to weather and with frequent need for strong waters, they move out in the pre-dawn darkness away to the lonely spaces beyond the flood banks, alone on the hinterland of the sea. They return in mid-morning mud-plastered, bloated with the wind, famished and hugely content with a couple of duck, an occasional goose, or nothing at all except the challenge of having been there. This is not a sport for fainthearts, dilettantes or fools.

Inland, their weatherproof counterparts fish summer and winter the network of man-made waterways linking back to Ouse, Nene and Welland. This is not knickerbocker country. There is no fly-fishing here. The anglers are miners, steelworkers, high-technology engineers, textile men whose tackle costs money that would turn a salmon-fisher pale.

They arrive in well-laden cars, well-provisioned too, ready to survive tempest or blizzard (which they often need to do). Many of them are match-fishermen. All are laconic but knowledgeable and deeply committed naturalists.

They look with contempt on those who see no fun in daylong hypothermia, crouched in the lee of a green storm-umbrella. They are human gazetteers of the man-made waterways, knowing the great drains by their dimensions — the Sixteen Foot, Twenty Foot, Forty Foot and Hundred Foot; the footage is more indicative than the county in locating them.

Their reward is contemplation of their keep-nets at the end of the day before the catch is returned to the water. Then several pints at some low-roofed, wind-dodging hostelry in friendly rivalry with the locals.

Such is the land that the presence of the Ouse made possible, the land from which the water was drawn away, the land which ever since has been sinking because dried earth shrinks, and which needs everlasting defence against floods, the land which fen tigers care for, and to which they gave the evocative name still scattered across those sheets of the maps which have no contours, Adventurers' Land.

Scattered there, too, are exotic un-English place names, fay-like and well-suited to places which rose above the waters — Guyhirn, Mepal, Manea, Elmeth, the Delphs and Guelphs and all the connotations of lodes and pumps and locks and cuts.

Across it all, herons beat their solitary flight. Their ancestors knew the land in days gone by, as did the ancestors of the robust men and women who live here now. Its flatness, its vistas and its cloudscapes have no endings.

Gigantic artefacts of God and man are dwarfed by its distances, the great cathedrals of Ely and Peterborough, the jagged grey sugar factories and food processing depots. The crops make glad the heart of man amid the roar and bustle of modernity, the thunderous road traffic, the clatter of crop-spraying helicopters, the glow and smoke palls of burning straw.

Yet still, for those with the eyes and the wish to see, nearly always, somewhere in view, are reeds shaken with the wind.

## Illustrations

# THE GREAT

Olney
Newport Pagnell
Bedford
Milton Keynes
Ouse
Great